Morning and Evening Prayer
from
The Book of Common Prayer
with permitted variations

C000063986

Morning and Evening Prayer from
The Book of Common Prayer
with permitted variations

Church House Publishing

Published by   Church House Publishing
                Church House
                Great Smith Street
                London SW1P 3NZ

Copyright ©   *The Archbishops' Council 2000*

                First published 2000

                0 7151 2030 1

Texts for local use: the arrangements which apply to local editions
of services cover reproduction on a non-commercial basis both
for a single occasion and for repeated use. Details are available
in the booklet *A Brief Guide to Liturgical Copyright* (see Copyright
Information in *Common Worship: Services and Prayers for the Church
of England* for further information).

Printed and bound by ArklePrint Ltd, Northampton
on 80 gsm Dutchman Ivory

Typeset in Gill Sans
by John Morgan and Shirley Thompson/Omnific
Designed by Derek Birdsall RDI

The material in this booklet is extracted from *Common Worship:
Services and Prayers for the Church of England*. It comprises:

¶   Schedule of Permitted Variations;
¶   Morning and Evening Prayer from *The BCP*;
¶   Prayers from *The BCP*;
¶   The Litany from *The BCP*;
¶   Further Canticles from *The BCP*;
¶   General Rules.

Pagination   This booklet has two sets of page numbers. The outer numbers
are the booklet's own page numbers, while the inner numbers
near the centre of most pages refer to the equivalent pages in
Common Worship: Services and Prayers for the Church of England.

Contents

Morning and Evening Prayer
from *The Book of Common Prayer*
with permitted variations (see page 22)

¶ *Opening Sentences*

Seasonal Sentences

General

O worship the Lord in the beauty of holiness: let the whole earth stand in awe of him. *Psalm 96.9*

God is Spirit: and they that worship him must worship him in spirit and in truth. *John 4.24*

Advent

The night is far spent, and the day is at hand: let us therefore cast off the works of darkness, and let us put on the armour of light. *Romans 13.12*

Christmas

Behold, I bring you good tidings of great joy which shall be to all people: for unto you is born in the city of David, a Saviour, which is Christ the Lord. *Luke 2.10,11*

Epiphany

From the rising of the sun even unto the going down of the same my name is great among the nations; and in every place incense is offered unto my name, and a pure offering: for my name is great among the nations, saith the Lord. *Malachi 1.11*

Lent

The sacrifices of God are a broken spirit: a broken and a contrite heart, O God, thou wilt not despise. *Psalm 51.17*

Passiontide

Is it nothing to you, all ye that pass by? Behold, and see if there be any sorrow like unto my sorrow. *Lamentations 1.12*

Good Friday

God commendeth his love toward us, in that, while we were yet sinners, Christ died for us. *Romans 5.8*

Easter Eve

Rest in the Lord and wait patiently for him; and he shall give thee thy heart's desire. *Psalm 37.7,4*

Easter

Blessed be the God and Father of our Lord Jesus Christ, who according to his great mercy hath begotten us again unto a living hope by the resurrection of Jesus Christ from the dead. *1 Peter 1.3*

Ascension Day

Seeing that we have a great high priest that is passed into the heavens, Jesus the Son of God, let us come boldly unto the throne of grace, that we may obtain mercy and find grace to help in time of need. *Hebrews 4.14,16*

Pentecost

The love of God hath been shed abroad in our hearts through the Holy Spirit which was given unto us. *Romans 5.5*

Trinity

God is love; and he that abideth in love abideth in God and God in him. *1 John 4.16*

Harvest

The earth is the Lord's, and the fullness thereof. *Psalm 24.1*

All Saints

Seeing we are compassed about with so great a cloud of witnesses, let us lay aside every weight, and the sin which doth so easily beset us, and let us run with patience the race that is set before us, looking unto Jesus, the author and perfecter of our faith. *Hebrews 12.1, 2*

Saints' Days

The righteous shall be had in everlasting remembrance; the memory of the just is blessed. *Psalm 112.6; Proverbs 10.7*

Time of Trouble

God is our hope and strength: a very present help in trouble. *Psalm 46.1*

Penitential Sentences

I will arise and go to my father, and will say unto him, Father, I have sinned against heaven, and before thee, and am no more worthy to be called thy son. *Luke 15.18, 19*

If we say that we have no sin, we deceive ourselves, and the truth is not in us: but if we confess our sins, he is faithful and just to forgive us our sins, and to cleanse us from all unrighteousness. *1 John 1.8, 9*

To the Lord our God belong mercies and forgivenesses, though we have rebelled against him: neither have we obeyed the voice of the Lord our God, to walk in his laws which he set before us.
Daniel 9.9, 10

Enter not into judgement with thy servant, O Lord; for in thy sight shall no man living be justified. *Psalm 143.2*

When the wicked man turneth away from his wickedness that he hath committed, and doeth that which is lawful and right, he shall save his soul alive. *Ezekiel 18.27*

I acknowledge my transgressions, and my sin is ever before me.
Psalm 51.3

Hide thy face from my sins, and blot out all mine iniquities.
Psalm 51.9

O Lord, correct me, but with judgement; not in thine anger, lest thou bring me to nothing. *Jeremiah 10.24; Psalm 6.1*

Repent ye; for the kingdom of heaven is at hand. *Matthew 3.2*

Rend your heart, and not your garments, and turn unto the Lord your God: for he is gracious and merciful, slow to anger, and of great kindness, and repenteth him of the evil. *Joel 2.13*

Morning Prayer from
The Book of Common Prayer

¶ *Introduction*

The minister may use a seasonal sentence before using one or more of the penitential sentences (see pages 1–3).

The minister introduces the service

Dearly beloved [brethren],
the Scripture moveth us in sundry places to acknowledge
and confess our manifold sins and wickedness;

[and that we should not dissemble nor cloak them before
the face of almighty God our heavenly Father;
but confess them with an humble, lowly, penitent and
obedient heart;
to the end that we may obtain forgiveness of the same
by his infinite goodness and mercy.
And although we ought at all times humbly to acknowledge
our sins before God;
yet ought we most chiefly so to do,
when we assemble and meet together
to render thanks for the great benefits that we have
received at his hands,
to set forth his most worthy praise,
to hear his most holy word,
and to ask those things which are requisite and necessary,
as well for the body as the soul.]

Wherefore I pray and beseech you,
as many as are here present,
to accompany me with a pure heart, and humble voice,
unto the throne of the heavenly grace, saying [after me]:

(or)

Beloved, we are come together in the presence of almighty God and of the whole company of heaven to offer unto him through our Lord Jesus Christ our worship and praise and thanksgiving; to make confession of our sins; to pray, as well for others as for ourselves, that we may know more truly the greatness of God's love and shew forth in our lives the fruits of his grace; and to ask on behalf of all men such things as their well-being doth require.

Wherefore let us kneel in silence, and remember God's presence with us now.

All **Almighty and most merciful Father,
we have erred, and strayed from thy ways like lost sheep.
We have followed too much the devices and desires
    of our own hearts.
We have offended against thy holy laws.
We have left undone those things
    which we ought to have done;
and we have done those things
    which we ought not to have done;
and there is no health in us.
But thou, O Lord, have mercy upon us, miserable offenders.
Spare thou them, O God, which confess their faults.
Restore thou them that are penitent;
according to thy promises declared unto mankind
    in Christ Jesu our Lord.
And grant, O most merciful Father, for his sake,
that we may hereafter live a godly, righteous, and sober life,
to the glory of thy holy name.
Amen.**

Almighty God, the Father of our Lord Jesus Christ,
who desireth not the death of a sinner,
but rather that he may turn from his wickedness and live;
and hath given power, and commandment, to his ministers
to declare and pronounce to his people, being penitent,
the absolution and remission of their sins:
he pardoneth and absolveth all them that truly repent
    and unfeignedly believe his holy gospel.
Wherefore let us beseech him to grant us true repentance,
    and his Holy Spirit,
that those things may please him which we do at this present;
and that the rest of our life hereafter may be pure and holy;
so that at the last we may come to his eternal joy;
through Jesus Christ our Lord.

All **Amen.**

or other ministers may say

Grant, we beseech thee, merciful Lord,
to thy faithful people pardon and peace,
that they may be cleansed from all their sins,
and serve thee with a quiet mind;
through Jesus Christ our Lord.

All **Amen.**

All **Our Father, which art in heaven,**
hallowed be thy name;
thy kingdom come;
thy will be done,
in earth as it is in heaven.
Give us this day our daily bread.
And forgive us our trespasses,
as we forgive them that trespass against us.
And lead us not into temptation;
but deliver us from evil.
For thine is the kingdom,
the power and the glory,
for ever and ever.
Amen.

¶ *Morning Prayer*

The introduction to the service (pages 4–6) is used on Sundays, and may be used on any occasion.

These responses are used

O Lord, open thou our lips
All **and our mouth shall shew forth thy praise.**

O God, make speed to save us.
All **O Lord, make haste to help us.**

Glory be to the Father, and to the Son,
and to the Holy Ghost;
All **as it was in the beginning, is now, and ever shall be,
world without end. Amen.**

Praise ye the Lord.
All **The Lord's name be praised.**

Venite, exultemus Domino

1   O come, let us sing unto the Lord :
let us heartily rejoice in the strength of our salvation.

2   Let us come before his presence with thanksgiving :
and shew ourselves glad in him with psalms.

3   For the Lord is a great God :
and a great King above all gods.

4   In his hand are all the corners of the earth :
and the strength of the hills is his also.

5   The sea is his, and he made it :
and his hands prepared the dry land.

6   O come, let us worship, and fall down :
and kneel before the Lord our Maker.

7   For he is the Lord our God :
and we are the people of his pasture, and the sheep of his hand.

[8 Today if ye will hear his voice, harden not your hearts :
 as in the provocation,
  and as in the day of temptation in the wilderness;

9 When your fathers tempted me :
 proved me, and saw my works.

10 Forty years long was I grieved with this generation, and said :
 It is a people that do err in their hearts,
  for they have not known my ways.

11 Unto whom I sware in my wrath :
 that they should not enter into my rest.]   *Psalm 95*

Glory be to the Father, and to the Son :
and to the Holy Ghost;
as it was in the beginning, is now, and ever shall be :
world without end. Amen.

Psalmody

At the end of each psalm these words are said or sung

Glory be to the Father, and to the Son :
and to the Holy Ghost;
as it was in the beginning, is now, and ever shall be :
world without end. Amen.

Old Testament Reading

Te Deum Laudamus

Either the Te Deum Laudamus (as follows) or Benedicite, omnia opera (pages 34–35) is said or sung.

We praise thee, O God; we acknowledge thee to be the Lord.
All the earth doth worship thee, the Father everlasting.
To thee all angels cry aloud, the heavens and all the powers therein.
To thee cherubin and seraphin continually do cry,
Holy, Holy, Holy, Lord God of Sabaoth;
Heaven and earth are full of the majesty of thy glory.
The glorious company of the apostles praise thee.
The goodly fellowship of the prophets praise thee.
The noble army of martyrs praise thee.
The holy Church throughout all the world doth acknowledge thee:
the Father of an infinite majesty;
thine honourable, true and only Son;
also the Holy Ghost the Comforter.

Thou art the King of glory, O Christ.
Thou art the everlasting Son of the Father.
When thou tookest upon thee to deliver man,
  thou didst not abhor the Virgin's womb.
When thou hadst overcome the sharpness of death,
  thou didst open the kingdom of heaven to all believers.
Thou sittest at the right hand of God, in the glory of the Father.
We believe that thou shalt come to be our judge.
We therefore pray thee, help thy servants,
  whom thou hast redeemed with thy precious blood.
Make them to be numbered with thy saints in glory everlasting.

O Lord, save thy people and bless thine heritage.
Govern them and lift them up for ever.
Day by day we magnify thee;
and we worship thy name, ever world without end.
Vouchsafe, O Lord, to keep us this day without sin.
O Lord, have mercy upon us, have mercy upon us.
O Lord, let thy mercy lighten upon us, as our trust is in thee.
O Lord, in thee have I trusted; let me never be confounded.

New Testament Reading

Either the Benedictus (as follows) or Jubilate Deo (Psalm 100, page 36) is said or sung.

1   Blessed be the Lord God of Israel :
    for he hath visited, and redeemed his people;

2   And hath raised up a mighty salvation for us :
    in the house of his servant David;

3   As he spake by the mouth of his holy Prophets :
    which have been since the world began;

4   That we should be saved from our enemies :
    and from the hands of all that hate us;

5   To perform the mercy promised to our forefathers :
    and to remember his holy covenant;

6   To perform the oath which he sware to our forefather Abraham :
    that he would give us,

7   That we being delivered out of the hands of our enemies :
    might serve him without fear,

8   In holiness and righteousness before him :
    all the days of our life.

9   And thou, child, shalt be called the Prophet of the Highest :
    for thou shalt go before the face of the Lord to prepare his ways;

10 To give knowledge of salvation unto his people :
    for the remission of their sins;

11 Through the tender mercy of our God :
    whereby the day-spring from on high hath visited us;

12 To give light to them that sit in darkness,
        and in the shadow of death :
    and to guide our feet into the way of peace.   *Luke 1.68-79*

    Glory be to the Father, and to the Son :
    and to the Holy Ghost;
    as it was in the beginning, is now, and ever shall be :
    world without end. Amen.

All **I believe in God the Father almighty,**
maker of heaven and earth:
and in Jesus Christ his only Son our Lord,
who was conceived by the Holy Ghost,
born of the Virgin Mary,
suffered under Pontius Pilate,
was crucified, dead, and buried.
He descended into hell;
the third day he rose again from the dead;
he ascended into heaven,
and sitteth on the right hand of God the Father almighty;
from thence he shall come to judge the quick and the dead.
I believe in the Holy Ghost;
the holy catholic Church;
the communion of saints;
the forgiveness of sins;
the resurrection of the body,
and the life everlasting.
Amen.

The Lord be with you.

All **And with thy spirit.**

Let us pray.

Lord, have mercy upon us.

All **Christ, have mercy upon us.**
Lord, have mercy upon us.

All **Our Father, which art in heaven,**
hallowed be thy name;
thy kingdom come;
thy will be done,
in earth as it is in heaven.
Give us this day our daily bread.
And forgive us our trespasses,
as we forgive them that trespass against us.
And lead us not into temptation;
but deliver us from evil. Amen.

O Lord, shew thy mercy upon us.

All **And grant us thy salvation.**

O Lord, save the Queen.

All **And mercifully hear us when we call upon thee.**

Endue thy ministers with righteousness.

All **And make thy chosen people joyful.**

O Lord, save thy people.

All **And bless thine inheritance.**

Give peace in our time, O Lord.

All **Because there is none other that fighteth for us,**
but only thou, O God.

O God, make clean our hearts within us.

All **And take not thy Holy Spirit from us.**

The Collect of the Day

The Collect for Peace

O God, who art the author of peace and lover of concord,
in knowledge of whom standeth our eternal life,
whose service is perfect freedom;
defend us thy humble servants in all assaults of our enemies;
that we, surely trusting in thy defence,
may not fear the power of any adversaries;
through the might of Jesus Christ our Lord.

All **Amen.**

The Collect for Grace

O Lord, our heavenly Father,
almighty and everlasting God,
who hast safely brought us to the beginning of this day;
defend us in the same with thy mighty power;
and grant that this day we fall into no sin,
neither run into any kind of danger,
but that all our doings may be ordered by thy governance,
to do always that is righteous in thy sight;
through Jesus Christ our Lord.

All **Amen.**

The order for the end of the service may include:

¶ *hymns or anthems*
¶ *a sermon*
¶ *further prayers (which may include prayers from pages 23–25)*

This prayer may be used to conclude the service

The grace of our Lord Jesus Christ,
and the love of God,
and the fellowship of the Holy Ghost,
be with us all evermore.

All **Amen.**

Evening Prayer from
The Book of Common Prayer

¶ *Introduction*

*The minister may use a seasonal sentence before using one or more of
the penitential sentences (see pages 1–3).*

The minister introduces the service

Dearly beloved [brethren],
the Scripture moveth us in sundry places to acknowledge
and confess our manifold sins and wickedness;

[and that we should not dissemble nor cloak them before
the face of almighty God our heavenly Father;
but confess them with an humble, lowly, penitent and
obedient heart;
to the end that we may obtain forgiveness of the same
by his infinite goodness and mercy.
And although we ought at all times humbly to acknowledge
our sins before God;
yet ought we most chiefly so to do,
when we assemble and meet together
to render thanks for the great benefits that we have
received at his hands,
to set forth his most worthy praise,
to hear his most holy word,
and to ask those things which are requisite and necessary,
as well for the body as the soul.]

Wherefore I pray and beseech you,
as many as are here present,
to accompany me with a pure heart, and humble voice,
unto the throne of the heavenly grace, saying [after me]:

(or)

Beloved, we are come together in the presence of almighty God and of the whole company of heaven to offer unto him through our Lord Jesus Christ our worship and praise and thanksgiving; to make confession of our sins; to pray, as well for others as for ourselves, that we may know more truly the greatness of God's love and shew forth in our lives the fruits of his grace; and to ask on behalf of all men such things as their well-being doth require.

Wherefore let us kneel in silence, and remember God's presence with us now.

All **Almighty and most merciful Father,**
we have erred, and strayed from thy ways like lost sheep.
We have followed too much the devices and desires
of our own hearts.
We have offended against thy holy laws.
We have left undone those things
which we ought to have done;
and we have done those things
which we ought not to have done;
and there is no health in us.
But thou, O Lord, have mercy upon us, miserable offenders.
Spare thou them, O God, which confess their faults.
Restore thou them that are penitent;
according to thy promises declared unto mankind
in Christ Jesu our Lord.
And grant, O most merciful Father, for his sake,
that we may hereafter live a godly, righteous, and sober life,
to the glory of thy holy name.
Amen.

Almighty God, the Father of our Lord Jesus Christ,
who desireth not the death of a sinner,
but rather that he may turn from his wickedness and live;
and hath given power, and commandment, to his ministers
to declare and pronounce to his people, being penitent,
the absolution and remission of their sins:
he pardoneth and absolveth all them that truly repent
    and unfeignedly believe his holy gospel.
Wherefore let us beseech him to grant us true repentance,
    and his Holy Spirit,
that those things may please him which we do at this present;
and that the rest of our life hereafter may be pure and holy;
so that at the last we may come to his eternal joy;
through Jesus Christ our Lord.

All **Amen.**

or other ministers may say

Grant, we beseech thee, merciful Lord,
to thy faithful people pardon and peace,
that they may be cleansed from all their sins,
and serve thee with a quiet mind;
through Jesus Christ our Lord.

All **Amen.**

All **Our Father, which art in heaven,**
    hallowed be thy name;
    thy kingdom come;
    thy will be done,
    in earth as it is in heaven.
    Give us this day our daily bread.
    And forgive us our trespasses,
    as we forgive them that trespass against us.
    And lead us not into temptation;
    but deliver us from evil.
    For thine is the kingdom,
    the power and the glory,
    for ever and ever.
    Amen.

¶ Evening Prayer

The introduction to the service (pages 14–16) is used on Sundays, and may be used on any occasion.

These responses are used

O Lord, open thou our lips
All **and our mouth shall shew forth thy praise.**

O God, make speed to save us.
All **O Lord, make haste to help us.**

Glory be to the Father, and to the Son,
and to the Holy Ghost;
All **as it was in the beginning, is now, and ever shall be,
world without end. Amen.**

Praise ye the Lord.
All **The Lord's name be praised.**

Psalmody

At the end of each psalm these words are said or sung

Glory be to the Father, and to the Son :
and to the Holy Ghost;
as it was in the beginning, is now, and ever shall be :
world without end. Amen.

Old Testament Reading

Either the Magnificat (as follows) or Cantate Domino
(Psalm 98, page 37) is said or sung.

1   My soul doth magnify the Lord :
    and my spirit hath rejoiced in God my Saviour.

2   For he hath regarded :
    the lowliness of his handmaiden.

3   For behold, from henceforth :
    all generations shall call me blessed.

4   For he that is mighty hath magnified me :
    and holy is his Name.

5   And his mercy is on them that fear him :
    throughout all generations.

6   He hath shewed strength with his arm :
    he hath scattered the proud in the imagination of their hearts.

7   He hath put down the mighty from their seat :
    and hath exalted the humble and meek.

8   He hath filled the hungry with good things :
    and the rich he hath sent empty away.

9   He remembering his mercy hath holpen his servant Israel :
    as he promised to our forefathers, Abraham and his seed for ever.

Luke 1.46-55

Glory be to the Father, and to the Son :
and to the Holy Ghost;
as it was in the beginning, is now, and ever shall be :
world without end. Amen.

New Testament Reading

*Either the Nunc dimittis (as follows) or Deus misereatur
(Psalm 67, page 38) is said or sung.*

1   Lord, now lettest thou thy servant depart in peace :
     according to thy word.

2   For mine eyes have seen :
     thy salvation;

3   Which thou hast prepared :
     before the face of all people;

4   To be a light to lighten the Gentiles :
     and to be the glory of thy people Israel.   *Luke 2.29-32*

Glory be to the Father, and to the Son :
and to the Holy Ghost;
as it was in the beginning, is now, and ever shall be :
world without end. Amen.

The Apostles' Creed

All   **I believe in God the Father almighty,
maker of heaven and earth:
and in Jesus Christ his only Son our Lord,
who was conceived by the Holy Ghost,
born of the Virgin Mary,
suffered under Pontius Pilate,
was crucified, dead, and buried.
He descended into hell;
the third day he rose again from the dead;
he ascended into heaven,
and sitteth on the right hand of God the Father almighty;
from thence he shall come to judge the quick and the dead.
I believe in the Holy Ghost;
the holy catholic Church;
the communion of saints;
the forgiveness of sins;
the resurrection of the body,
and the life everlasting.
Amen.**

The Lord be with you.

All **And with thy spirit.**

Let us pray.

Lord, have mercy upon us.

All **Christ, have mercy upon us.**
Lord, have mercy upon us.

All **Our Father, which art in heaven,**
hallowed be thy name;
thy kingdom come;
thy will be done,
in earth as it is in heaven.
Give us this day our daily bread.
And forgive us our trespasses,
as we forgive them that trespass against us.
And lead us not into temptation;
but deliver us from evil. Amen.

O Lord, shew thy mercy upon us.

All **And grant us thy salvation.**

O Lord, save the Queen.

All **And mercifully hear us when we call upon thee.**

Endue thy ministers with righteousness.

All **And make thy chosen people joyful.**

O Lord, save thy people.

All **And bless thine inheritance.**

Give peace in our time, O Lord.

All **Because there is none other that fighteth for us,**
but only thou, O God.

O God, make clean our hearts within us.

All **And take not thy Holy Spirit from us.**

Three Collects are said.

The Collect of the Day

The Collect for Peace

O God, from whom all holy desires, all good counsels,
　and all just works do proceed;
give unto thy servants that peace which the world cannot give;
that both, our hearts may be set to obey thy commandments,
and also that, by thee,
we being defended from the fear of our enemies
may pass our time in rest and quietness;
through the merits of Jesus Christ our Saviour.

All　**Amen.**

The Collect for Aid against all Perils

Lighten our darkness, we beseech thee, O Lord;
and by thy great mercy defend us
　from all perils and dangers of this night;
for the love of thy only Son, our Saviour, Jesus Christ.

All　**Amen.**

The order for the end of the service may include:

¶　*hymns or anthems*
¶　*a sermon*
¶　*further prayers (which may include prayers from pages 23–25)*

This prayer may be used to conclude the service

The grace of our Lord Jesus Christ,
and the love of God,
and the fellowship of the Holy Ghost,
be with us all evermore.

All　**Amen.**

Schedule of Permitted Variations

to the *Book of Common Prayer* Orders for Morning and Evening Prayer where these occur in *Common Worship*

1   All or part of the material before 'O Lord, open thou our lips' may be omitted, at least on weekdays.

2   The minister may use a seasonal sentence before using one of the penitential sentences with which the service begins.

3   The minister may use an abbreviated form of the Bidding, 'Dearly beloved brethren …', or the form on pages 5 and 15 may be used.

4   When the officiating minister is not a priest, an authorized prayer for absolution in the 'us' form or else the Collect for Trinity 21 in *The Book of Common Prayer* is said by the minister in place of the prayer for absolution printed in *The Book of Common Prayer*.

5   The whole of the Gloria Patri, together with the words 'Praise ye the Lord' that follow, may be said or sung by the entire congregation, in which case the final response, 'The Lord's name be praised', may be omitted.

6   At Morning Prayer, verses 8 to 11 of the Venite may be omitted except in Lent. The Easter Anthems (page 33) may be used in place of the Venite throughout Eastertide.

7   Other prayers of intercession and thanksgiving may be used in addition to or in place of the five prayers printed at the end of the Order in *The Book of Common Prayer*.

8   Hymns may be sung at suitable points in the service, silence may be kept after the readings, a sermon may be preached and the service may end with a blessing.

For General Rules, see page 39.

Prayers from
The Book of Common Prayer

A Prayer for the Queen's Majesty

O Lord our heavenly Father,
high and mighty, King of kings, Lord of lords, the only Ruler of princes,
who dost from thy throne behold all the dwellers upon earth;
most heartily we beseech thee with thy favour
    to behold our most gracious Sovereign Lady, *Queen Elizabeth*;
and so replenish her with the grace of thy Holy Spirit,
that she may alway incline to thy will, and walk in thy way:
endue her plenteously with heavenly gifts;
grant her in health and wealth long to live;
strengthen her that she may vanquish and overcome all her enemies;
and finally, after this life, she may attain everlasting joy and felicity;
through Jesus Christ our Lord.

All   **Amen.**

A Collect for the Queen

Almighty and everlasting God,
we are taught by thy holy Word,
    that the hearts of kings are in thy rule and governance,
and that thou dost dispose and turn them
    as it seemeth best to thy godly wisdom:
we humbly beseech thee so to dispose and govern the heart of
    Elizabeth thy Servant, our *Queen* and Governor,
that, in all her thoughts, words, and works,
she may ever seek thy honour and glory,
and study to preserve thy people committed to her charge,
    in wealth, peace, and godliness:
grant this, O merciful Father, for thy dear Son's sake,
    Jesus Christ our Lord.

All   **Amen.**

A Prayer for the Royal Family

Almighty God, the fountain of all goodness,
we humbly beseech thee to bless *Elizabeth the Queen Mother*,
Philip Duke of Edinburgh, Charles Prince of Wales,
and all the Royal Family.
Endue them with thy Holy Spirit;
enrich them with thy heavenly grace;
prosper them with all happiness;
and bring them to thine everlasting kingdom;
through Jesus Christ our Lord.

All **Amen.**

A Prayer for the Clergy and People

Almighty and everlasting God,
who alone workest great marvels,
send down upon our bishops and curates,
and all congregations committed to their charge,
the healthful spirit of thy grace;
and that they may truly please thee,
pour upon them the continual dew of thy blessing.
Grant this, O Lord,
for the honour of our advocate and mediator, Jesus Christ.

All **Amen.**

A Prayer of St Chrysostom

Almighty God,
who hast given us grace at this time
with one accord to make our common supplications unto thee;
and dost promise
that when two or three are gathered together in thy Name
thou wilt grant their requests:
fulfil now, O Lord, the desires and petitions of thy servants,
as may be most expedient for them;
granting us in this world knowledge of thy truth,
and in the world to come life everlasting.

All **Amen.**

Almighty God, Father of all mercies,
we thine unworthy servants
    do give thee most humble and hearty thanks
for all thy goodness and loving-kindness to us and to all men;
* [*particularly to those who desire now to offer up their praises
    and thanksgivings for thy late mercies vouchsafed unto them.*]
We bless thee for our creation, preservation,
    and all the blessings of this life;
but above all for thine inestimable love
in the redemption of the world by our Lord Jesus Christ,
for the means of grace, and for the hope of glory.
And we beseech thee, give us that due sense of all thy mercies,
that our hearts may be unfeignedly thankful,
and that we shew forth thy praise, not only with our lips,
    but in our lives;
by giving up ourselves to thy service,
and by walking before thee in holiness and righteousness
    all our days;
through Jesus Christ our Lord,
to whom with thee and the Holy Ghost
be all honour and glory, world without end.

All   **Amen.**

  * *This to be said when any that have been prayed for
    desire to return praise.*

The Litany from
The Book of Common Prayer

O God the Father of heaven:
have mercy upon us miserable sinners.

All **O God the Father of heaven:**
have mercy upon us miserable sinners.

O God the Son, Redeemer of the world:
have mercy upon us miserable sinners.

All **O God the Son, Redeemer of the world:**
have mercy upon us miserable sinners.

O God the Holy Ghost, proceeding from the Father and the Son:
have mercy upon us miserable sinners.

All **O God the Holy Ghost,**
proceeding from the Father and the Son:
have mercy upon us miserable sinners.

O holy, blessed, and glorious Trinity, three Persons and one God:
have mercy upon us miserable sinners.

All **O holy, blessed, and glorious Trinity,**
three Persons and one God:
have mercy upon us miserable sinners.

Remember not, Lord, our offences,
nor the offences of our forefathers;
neither take thou vengeance of our sins:
spare us, good Lord, spare thy people,
whom thou hast redeemed with thy most precious blood,
and be not angry with us for ever.

All **Spare us, good Lord.**

From all evil and mischief;
from sin, from the crafts and assaults of the devil;
from thy wrath, and from everlasting damnation,

All   **good Lord, deliver us.**

From all blindness of heart;
from pride, vain-glory, and hypocrisy;
from envy, hatred, and malice, and all uncharitableness,

All   **good Lord, deliver us.**

From fornication, and all other deadly sin;
and from all the deceits of the world, the flesh, and the devil,

All   **good Lord, deliver us.**

From lightning and tempest;
from plague, pestilence, and famine;
from battle and murder, and from sudden death,

All   **good Lord, deliver us.**

From all sedition, privy conspiracy, and rebellion;
from all false doctrine, heresy, and schism;
from hardness of heart,
    and contempt of thy Word and Commandment,

All   **good Lord, deliver us.**

By the mystery of thy holy Incarnation;
by thy holy Nativity and Circumcision;
by thy Baptism, Fasting, and Temptation,

All   **good Lord, deliver us.**

By thine Agony and bloody Sweat;
by thy Cross and Passion;
by thy precious Death and Burial;
by thy glorious Resurrection and Ascension;
and by the coming of the Holy Ghost,

All   **good Lord, deliver us.**

In all time of our tribulation; in all time of our wealth;
in the hour of death, and in the day of judgement,

All   **good Lord, deliver us.**

We sinners do beseech thee to hear us, O Lord God;
and that it may please thee to rule and govern
thy holy Church universal in the right way,

All **we beseech thee to hear us, good Lord.**

That it may please thee to keep and strengthen
in the true worshipping of thee,
in righteousness and holiness of life,
thy Servant *Elizabeth*, our most gracious *Queen* and Governor,

All **we beseech thee to hear us, good Lord.**

That it may please thee to rule her heart in thy faith, fear, and love,
and that she may evermore have affiance in thee,
and ever seek thy honour and glory,

All **we beseech thee to hear us, good Lord.**

That it may please thee to be her defender and keeper,
giving her the victory over all her enemies,

All **we beseech thee to hear us, good Lord.**

That it may please thee to bless and preserve
Elizabeth the Queen Mother,
Philip Duke of Edinburgh, Charles Prince of Wales,
and all the Royal Family,

All **we beseech thee to hear us, good Lord.**

That it may please thee to illuminate
all Bishops, Priests, and Deacons,
with true knowledge and understanding of thy Word;
and that both by their preaching and living
they may set it forth and shew it accordingly,

All **we beseech thee to hear us, good Lord.**

That it may please thee to endue the Lords of the Council,
and all the Nobility,†
with grace, wisdom, and understanding,

All **we beseech thee to hear us, good Lord.**

That it may please thee to bless and keep the Magistrates,
giving them grace to execute justice, and to maintain truth,

All **we beseech thee to hear us, good Lord.**

That it may please thee to bless and keep all thy people,

All **we beseech thee to hear us, good Lord.**

† *or* the High Court of Parliament and all the Ministers of the Crown

That it may please thee to give to all nations
    unity, peace, and concord,

All **we beseech thee to hear us, good Lord.**

That it may please thee to give us an heart to love and dread thee,
and diligently to live after thy commandments,

All **we beseech thee to hear us, good Lord.**

That it may please thee to give to all thy people increase of grace,
to hear meekly thy Word, and to receive it with pure affection,
and to bring forth the fruits of the Spirit,

All **we beseech thee to hear us, good Lord.**

That it may please thee to bring into the way of truth
    all such as have erred, and are deceived,

All **we beseech thee to hear us, good Lord.**

That it may please thee to strengthen such as do stand;
and to comfort and help the weak-hearted;
and to raise up them that fall;
and finally to beat down Satan under our feet,

All **we beseech thee to hear us, good Lord.**

That it may please thee to succour, help, and comfort
all that are in danger, necessity, and tribulation,

All **we beseech thee to hear us, good Lord.**

That it may please thee to preserve all that travel
    by land or by water, †
all women labouring of child, all sick persons, and young children;
and to shew thy pity upon all prisoners and captives,

All **we beseech thee to hear us, good Lord.**

That it may please thee to defend, and provide for,
    the fatherless children, and widows,
and all that are desolate and oppressed,

All **we beseech thee to hear us, good Lord.**

That it may please thee to have mercy upon all men,

All **we beseech thee to hear us, good Lord.**

† *or* **by land or air or water**

That it may please thee to forgive our enemies,
persecutors, and slanderers,
and to turn their hearts,

All **we beseech thee to hear us, good Lord.**

That it may please thee to give and preserve to our use
the kindly fruits of the earth,
so as in due time we may enjoy them,

All **we beseech thee to hear us, good Lord.**

That it may please thee to give us true repentance;
to forgive us all our sins, negligences, and ignorances;
and to endue us with the grace of thy Holy Spirit,
to amend our lives according to thy holy Word,

All **we beseech thee to hear us, good Lord.**

Son of God: we beseech thee to hear us.

All **Son of God: we beseech thee to hear us.**

O Lamb of God: that takest away the sins of the world,

All **grant us thy peace.**

O Lamb of God: that takest away the sins of the world,

All **have mercy upon us.**

O Christ, hear us.

All **O Christ, hear us.**

Lord, have mercy upon us.

All **Lord, have mercy upon us.**

Christ, have mercy upon us.

All **Christ, have mercy upon us.**

Lord, have mercy upon us.

All **Lord, have mercy upon us.**

All **Our Father, which art in heaven,**
hallowed be thy name;
thy kingdom come;
thy will be done,
in earth as it is in heaven.
Give us this day our daily bread.
And forgive us our trespasses,
as we forgive them that trespass against us.
And lead us not into temptation;
but deliver us from evil.
Amen.

O Lord, deal not with us after our sins.

All **Neither reward us after our iniquities.**

Let us pray.

O God, merciful Father,
that despisest not the sighing of a contrite heart,
nor the desire of such as be sorrowful:
mercifully assist our prayers that we make before thee
    in all our troubles and adversities, whensoever they oppress us;
and graciously hear us, that those evils,
which the craft and subtilty of the devil or man worketh against us,
be brought to nought,
and by the providence of thy goodness they may be dispersed;
that we thy servants, being hurt by no persecutions,
may evermore give thanks unto thee in thy holy Church;
through Jesus Christ our Lord.

All **O Lord, arise, help us, and deliver us for thy Name's sake.**

O God, we have heard with our ears,
and our fathers have declared unto us,
the noble works that thou didst in their days,
and in the old time before them.

All **O Lord, arise, help us, and deliver us for thine honour.**

Glory be to the Father, and to the Son
and to the Holy Ghost;

All **as it was in the beginning, is now, and ever shall be**
world without end. Amen.

From our enemies defend us, O Christ.

All **Graciously look upon our afflictions.**

Pitifully behold the sorrows of our hearts.

All **Mercifully forgive the sins of thy people.**

Favourably with mercy hear our prayers.

All **O Son of David, have mercy upon us.**

Both now and ever vouchsafe to hear us, O Christ.

All **Graciously hear us, O Christ;**
graciously hear us, O Lord Christ.

O Lord, let thy mercy be shewed upon us;

All **as we do put our trust in thee.**

Let us pray.

We humbly beseech thee, O Father,
mercifully to look upon our infirmities;
and for the glory of thy Name
turn from us all those evils that we most righteously have deserved;
and grant that in all our troubles
we may put our whole trust and confidence in thy mercy,
and evermore serve thee in holiness and pureness of living,
to thy honour and glory;
through our only Mediator and Advocate,
Jesus Christ our Lord.

All **Amen.**

Almighty God,
who hast given us grace at this time
with one accord to make our common supplications unto thee;
and dost promise
that when two or three are gathered together in thy Name
thou wilt grant their requests:
fulfil now, O Lord, the desires and petitions of thy servants,
as may be most expedient for them;
granting us in this world knowledge of thy truth,
and in the world to come life everlasting.

All **Amen.**

The grace of our Lord Jesus Christ,
and the love of God,
and the fellowship of the Holy Ghost,
be with us all evermore.   *2 Corinthians 13.13*

All **Amen.**

Further Canticles from
The Book of Common Prayer

Morning Prayer

The Easter Anthems

1   Christ our passover is sacrificed for us :
therefore let us keep the feast;

2   Not with the old leaven,
     nor with the leaven of malice and wickedness :
but with the unleavened bread of sincerity and truth.

I Corinthians 5.7b, 8

3   Christ being raised from the dead dieth no more :
death hath no more dominion over him.

4   For in that he died, he died unto sin once :
but in that he liveth, he liveth unto God.

5   Likewise reckon ye also yourselves to be dead indeed unto sin :
but alive unto God, through Jesus Christ our Lord.   *Romans 6.9-11*

6   Christ is risen from the dead :
and become the first fruits of them that slept.

7   For since by man came death :
by man came also the resurrection of the dead.

8   For as in Adam all die :
even so in Christ shall all be made alive.   *I Corinthians 15.20-22*

   Glory be to the Father, and to the Son :
and to the Holy Ghost;
as it was in the beginning, is now, and ever shall be :
world without end. Amen.

1   O all ye Works of the Lord, bless ye the Lord :
    praise him, and magnify him for ever.

2   O ye Angels of the Lord, bless ye the Lord :
    praise him, and magnify him for ever.

3   O ye Heavens, bless ye the Lord :
    praise him, and magnify him for ever.

4   O ye Waters that be above the Firmament, bless ye the Lord :
    praise him, and magnify him for ever.

5   O all ye Powers of the Lord, bless ye the Lord :
    praise him, and magnify him for ever.

6   O ye Sun and Moon, bless ye the Lord :
    praise him, and magnify him for ever.

7   O ye Stars of Heaven, bless ye the Lord :
    praise him, and magnify him for ever.

8   O ye Showers and Dew, bless ye the Lord :
    praise him, and magnify him for ever.

9   O ye Winds of God, bless ye the Lord :
    praise him, and magnify him for ever.

10 O ye Fire and Heat, bless ye the Lord :
    praise him, and magnify him for ever.

11 O ye Winter and Summer, bless ye the Lord :
    praise him, and magnify him for ever.

12 O ye Dews and Frosts, bless ye the Lord :
    praise him, and magnify him for ever.

13 O ye Frost and Cold, bless ye the Lord :
    praise him, and magnify him for ever.

14 O ye Ice and Snow, bless ye the Lord :
    praise him, and magnify him for ever.

15 O ye Nights and Days, bless ye the Lord :
    praise him, and magnify him for ever.

16 O ye Light and Darkness, bless ye the Lord :
    praise him, and magnify him for ever.

17 O ye Lightnings and Clouds, bless ye the Lord :
    praise him, and magnify him for ever.

18   O let the Earth bless the Lord :
      yea, let it praise him, and magnify him for ever.

19   O ye Mountains and Hills, bless ye the Lord :
      praise him, and magnify him for ever.

20   O all ye Green Things upon the Earth, bless ye the Lord :
      praise him, and magnify him for ever.

21   O ye Wells, bless ye the Lord :
      praise him, and magnify him for ever.

22   O ye Seas and Floods, bless ye the Lord :
      praise him, and magnify him for ever.

23   O ye Whales, and all that move in the Waters, bless ye the Lord :
      praise him, and magnify him for ever.

24   O all ye Fowls of the Air, bless ye the Lord :
      praise him, and magnify him for ever.

25   O all ye Beasts and Cattle, bless ye the Lord :
      praise him, and magnify him for ever.

26   O ye Children of Men, bless ye the Lord :
      praise him, and magnify him for ever.

27   O let Israel bless the Lord :
      praise him, and magnify him for ever.

28   O ye Priests of the Lord, bless ye the Lord :
      praise him, and magnify him for ever.

29   O ye Servants of the Lord, bless ye the Lord :
      praise him, and magnify him for ever.

30   O ye Spirits and Souls of the Righteous, bless ye the Lord :
      praise him, and magnify him for ever.

31   O ye holy and humble Men of heart, bless ye the Lord :
      praise him, and magnify him for ever.

32   O Ananias, Azarias and Misael, bless ye the Lord :
      praise him, and magnify him for ever.

The Song of the Three Holy Children 35-66

Glory be to the Father, and to the Son :
and to the Holy Ghost;
as it was in the beginning, is now, and ever shall be :
world without end. Amen.

1   O be joyful in the Lord, all ye lands :
serve the Lord with gladness,
       and come before his presence with a song.

2   Be ye sure that the Lord he is God :
it is he that hath made us, and not we ourselves;
       we are his people, and the sheep of his pasture.

3   O go your way into his gates with thanksgiving,
       and into his courts with praise :
be thankful unto him, and speak good of his Name.

4   For the Lord is gracious, his mercy is everlasting :
and his truth endureth from generation to generation.   *Psalm 100*

Glory be to the Father, and to the Son :
and to the Holy Ghost;
as it was in the beginning, is now, and ever shall be :
world without end. Amen.

Evening Prayer

Cantate Domino

1   O sing unto the Lord a new song :
for he hath done marvellous things.

2   With his own right hand, and with his holy arm :
hath he gotten himself the victory.

3   The Lord declared his salvation :
his righteousness hath he openly shewed in the sight of the heathen.

4   He hath remembered his mercy and truth
      toward the house of Israel :
and all the ends of the world have seen the salvation of our God.

5   Shew yourselves joyful unto the Lord, all ye lands :
sing, rejoice, and give thanks.

6   Praise the Lord upon the harp :
sing to the harp with a psalm of thanksgiving.

7   With trumpets also and shawms :
O shew yourselves joyful before the Lord the King.

8   Let the sea make a noise, and all that therein is :
the round world, and they that dwell therein.

9   Let the floods clap their hands,
      and let the hills be joyful together before the Lord :
for he cometh to judge the earth.

10   With righteousness shall he judge the world :
and the people with equity.   *Psalm 98*

Glory be to the Father, and to the Son :
and to the Holy Ghost;
as it was in the beginning, is now, and ever shall be :
world without end. Amen.

1   God be merciful unto us, and bless us :
     and shew us the light of his countenance, and be merciful unto us:

2   That thy way may be known upon earth :
     thy saving health among all nations.

3   Let the people praise thee, O God :
     yea, let all the people praise thee.

4   O let the nations rejoice and be glad :
     for thou shalt judge the folk righteously,
       and govern the nations upon earth.

5   Let the people praise thee, O God :
     yea, let all the people praise thee.

6   Then shall the earth bring forth her increase :
     and God, even our own God, shall give us his blessing.

7   God shall bless us :
     and all the ends of the world shall fear him.   *Psalm 67*

Glory be to the Father, and to the Son :
and to the Holy Ghost;
as it was in the beginning, is now, and ever shall be :
world without end. Amen.

General Rules for Regulating Authorized Forms of Service

1   Any reference in authorized provision to the use of hymns shall be construed as including the use of texts described as songs, chants, canticles.

2   If occasion requires, hymns may be sung at points other than those indicated in particular forms of service. Silence may be kept at points other than those indicated in particular forms of service.

3   Where rubrics indicate that a text is to be 'said' this must be understood to include 'or sung' and vice versa.

4   Where parts of a service make use of well-known and traditional texts, other translations or versions, particularly when used in musical compositions, may be used.

5   Local custom may be established and followed in respect of posture but regard should be had to indications in Notes attached to authorized forms of service that a particular posture is appropriate for some parts of that form of service.

6   On any occasion when the text of an alternative service authorized under the provisions of Canon B 2 provides for the Lord's Prayer to be said or sung, it may be used in the form included in *The Book of Common Prayer* or in either of the two other forms included in services in *Common Worship*. The further text included in Prayers for Various Occasions (page 106 in *Common Worship: Services and Prayers for the Church of England*) may be used on suitable occasions.

7   Normally on any occasion only one Collect is used.

8   At Baptisms, Confirmations, Ordinations and Marriages which take place on Principal Feasts, other Principal Holy Days and on Sundays of Advent, Lent and Easter, within the Celebration of the Holy Communion, the Readings of the day are used and the Collect of the Day is said, unless the bishop directs otherwise.

9   The Collects and Lectionary in *Common Worship* may, optionally, be used in conjunction with the days included in the Calendar of *The Book of Common Prayer*, notwithstanding any difference in the title or name of a Sunday, Holy Day or other observance included in both Calendars.

Authorization

¶ The following services and other material in *Common Worship: Services and Prayers for the Church of England* are taken from *The Book of Common Prayer:*

   ¶ Texts from Morning and Evening Prayer in *The Book of Common Prayer*

   ¶ Prayers from *The Book of Common Prayer* in Prayers for Various Occasions

   ¶ The Litany from *The Book of Common Prayer*

   ¶ Canticles from *The Book of Common Prayer*

   The Church of England (Worship and Doctrine) Measure 1974 provides that the forms of service contained in *The Book of Common Prayer* shall continue to be available for use in the Church of England.

¶ The following material is authorized pursuant to Canon B 2 of the Canons of the Church of England for use until further resolution of the General Synod:

   ¶ Schedule of permitted variations to *The Book of Common Prayer* Orders for Morning and Evening Prayer where these occur in *Common Worship*

   ¶ General Rules for Regulating Authorized Forms of Service

¶ The following services comply with the Schedule of permitted variations to *The Book of Common Prayer* Orders for Morning and Evening Prayer where these occur in *Common Worship*:

   ¶ Morning Prayer from *The Book of Common Prayer* with permitted variations

   ¶ Evening Prayer from *The Book of Common Prayer* with permitted variations

Acknowledgements

The publisher gratefully acknowledges permission to reproduce copyright material in this book.

Published sources include the following:

Cambridge University Press: Extracts from *The Book of Common Prayer*, the rights in which are vested in the Crown, are reproduced by permission of the Crown's Patentee, Cambridge University Press.

The Archbishops' Council of the Church of England: *The Prayer Book as Proposed in 1928* which is copyright © The Archbishops' Council of the Church of England.